In Celebration of the Ordinary

(and the extraordinary!)

Neeta Nayak

All author profits are donated to organizations fighting hunger. Because YOU choose to read these pages it helps feed someone in need. Every purchase supports hunger relief.

Neeta Nayak
neetan88@icloud.com

FIRST EDITION
Edited and formatted by: Richard Kushmaul
Cover Design: Ananya Rao

ISBN: 979-8-9943371-0-3

About The Cover

The cover reflects the poetry collection's central theme of finding beauty in everyday moments. The birds flying across a soft sky felt right for poems that explore freedom and simple joys. The watercolor clouds give it a dreamlike quality that matches the contemplative nature of the writing. Using a handwritten style for the title adds warmth and makes it feel personal, like the intimate stories inside. The simplicity of the design lets the main idea come through clearly, showing how ordinary life holds extraordinary moments worth celebrating. The sunlight spreading across the top brings in that sense of hope that runs through the entire collection.

-Ananya Rao

Index

Preface

Neeta Nayak is a physician with a poetic heart. She recognizes the healing power of poetry and admits to living with "optimistic passion." When Neeta reached out for information about the Mockingbird Poetry Society, I could almost hear the "click" that comes when you meet someone who you could talk with for hours, without effort, with one topic leading to another. I continue to be impressed by her energy, her vitality, her accomplishments, and her writing. Neeta's poetry collection, In *Celebration of the Ordinary (and the extraordinary!)* is filled with variety and meaning. Her poetry ranges from playful to serious, from creating a new word to explain the sky's color (between pink and orange) to struggles of life and death. Some poems celebrate friends and colleagues who have inspired and impressed her. Some come from memories of special people or special moments. Some were born from everyday experiences. Neeta allows a rainbow to speak, to tell us to "Live life boldly, brightly, benevolently, brilliantly!" I will listen the next time I see a rainbow.

Neeta enjoys the art of putting thoughts into writing and she is ready and waiting for the next inspiration. As she admits in one poem, "I gaze upon humanity and await more stories!" In this collection of poetry, you have the opportunity to enter Neeta's world and her optimistic youthfulness will charm you.

- Beth Turner Ayers
Past President, Mockingbird Poetry Society

Foreword

I am filled with wonder-at sunshine and starlight, the reflection of mountains and trees in still waters, the raging sea, the storms of life, the wind in my hair. At the hypocrisy of human nature and the beauty of a centenarian's smile. At the tantrums of a toddler-or a teen. At the poverty of an existence and the love of one human for another. At behavior that defines humanness and that which defies imagination. All of it.

Poetry feels like a naturally occurring language, flowing from both spectating life and participating in it.

Some of these poems were born during COVID; others followed later. For years, I would "think" poetic thoughts on the solitary walks to and from middle and high school, but I was too embarrassed to write them down. In my young unseasoned mind, poetry belonged only to the greatest writers-not to ordinary people like me. It never occurred to me that the mind can do extraordinary things even in an ordinary person, things that may never garner a second glance.

So although I technically "wrote" many of these poems during COVID-the only time in my entire career when I could work from home-I was really preserving thoughts I'd THINKED in childhood! I took walks, sat on quiet park benches, and used social distancing and solitude to finally hold onto them.

Some of these poems rhyme, and I let them. They may appeal to the non-poets. Some don't rhyme at all and look more like prose - that is the newer version of me, attempting to fall in line with today's poetry culture. Or at least my observation of it.

My identity arises from my personal life-as a granddaughter to an extraordinary grandmother who loved me more than life itself, and as a mother who loves her children the same way. In between, are the real-life influencers - my husband, parents, sister, nieces, nephews, cousins, aunts, uncles, cats, friends who are all very dear to me. It also comes from my professional life as a geriatrician and palliative medicine physician. It is a sincere privilege to be a confidante to those whose ailments define their daily lives and who still possess the power to smile, forgive, and endure. I teach, but I learn far more. The many influences that shape a person inevitably flow into their world of words, and my mind is no different.

Poetry gives me the confidence and courage to make my life whole.

I hope you enjoy reading this collection. If a poem doesn't resonate, skip ahead-you're likely to find another that speaks to you. This book is a celebration of the ordinary and the extraordinary life most of us are navigating-guided by heart, spirit and occasionally a sense of humor.

Chapter 1: Anatomy of Hope

Gas or Petrol – Neither a Rose!

I remember the first time
my father filled up the small gas tank
of his brand-new vespa scooter
in a place called a petrol bunk,
and it smelt of burnt firewood,
perspiring human flesh
and the hope for a better life.

Me, a little girl of five
standing between his driver's seat and front wheel
feeling the humming engine under my toes.
The passenger seat holding my mother,
who was holding my baby sister in her lap.

Four fine people, aged between
three months and thirty-three
riding on a scooter barely bigger than a bicycle,
happy about our freedom
of mobility on the bumpy
potholed city road.

I wondered why petrol is called gas in America,
when the rest of the world mostly used the term
to describe the wind generated
in the gastrointestinal system.

I realized - a petrol bunk,
or gas station by any other name,
would, unlike a rose,
smell just as sharp.

The aroma of life in motion!

A Hello and a Goodbye

The plane passes through a massive cloud
It's silvery body shaking from side to side
Turbulence stirred the cloud without sound
Passengers tremulous on this rough ride.

Return to your seat
Fasten your seatbelt
Pilot says without missing a beat
Passengers ignore the safety warning dealt.

Fire drills we do at work
Screeching alarms that wake up the dead
We learn to ignore this perk
Because we develop alarm fatigue quicker than said.

The plane rises above the cloudy mass
That looks like a melting glacier in the sky
"Even this shall pass"
Life is nothing but hope sandwiched between
a hello and a goodbye!

A "girl" child, NO less!

(The story of my grandmother born over a century ago in southern India at a time when girls were considered a burden, an expense and boys were seen as an asset to the family, told in the style of a prose-poem. I recited this at the SAWPNA - South Asian women physicians of North America conference in May 2024.)

She was born in 1917
A girl child, no concept of tween or teen
Nobody asked her, "So what do you want to be when you grow up?"
She was a girl…… merely staying alive to see adulthood was a step up.

A child bride or a teenage wife for sure
It was guaranteed for girls, rich or poor
A mother maybe when she was herself a child
Her choices were nonexistent
OH NO a girl could not run wild
OH NO a girl could not run wild.

Her mother despaired at her birth
Her father wept silently-Another big dowry to put forth
Certainly, another mouth to feed
What good is a girl except to breed?

She was born in India at a time
When being born a girlchild was a crime
She said her parents had been kind, really,
She'd been spared female infanticide, she smiled sadly.

She wanted more education
Instead, she added babies to the population
All her life was spent cooking, supervising the kitchen like a food proctor
But all she desperately wanted was to be a doctor.

……. What if she'd been born in 1970 instead?
When a girl's value was a bit ahead
She'd be asked-
"So, what do you want to be when you grow up?"
See, you'd have had options-Wasn't that a huge step up?

I asked my Annamma - why would YOU want to be a doctor?
Why not a banker, a lawyer or an engineer?
And she said- Doctors have the very best job
People tell you things that they would never ever tell Tom, Dick or Bob.

Doctors get to do the coolest stuff
Like listening to beating hearts and placing a blood pressure cuff
Listening to the life breath inside another human being
Finding solutions to
life-threatening problems that are freeing.

What privilege it is to wear a pristine white coat?
To look into the gateway that's one's THROAT
To hold a marvelous instrument called a stethoscope
To give a suffering person, a glimmer of hope.

Do you realize that a doctor maybe someone's only friend
A confidante you can never offend?
My Annamma said- That is what I wanted to be
I wanted the skill to make someone pain free!

I want for you what I could never have had
A real childhood, a career that makes you glad
Not be passed like an unwanted toy from father to husband to son, not merely someone's wife,
I want you to have courage to live your OWN life.

And so, I became a medicine woman
To fulfil Annamma's and my dreams, that of many with passion
A life of studying 14 hours a day
A life of working 14 hours a day to make some hay.

But somewhere along the road I fell into a slump
So many problems seemed to clump
Battling insurance denials and prior authorizations
Keeping up with corporate mergers and staff turnovers.

Juggling children and teenage impertinence
Soaring malpractice premiums and charting in permanence
Falling reimbursements, fearing losing independence
Oh no I thought, am I losing my mature tolerance?

As I fell into this rabbit hole of spiraling despair
My Annamma suddenly appeared in a dream so fair -
Looking wrathfully fierce like Goddess Durga Devi
Riding an enraged tiger- I woke up sweating, profusely!

She raved and she ranted and shook furiously
Would you rather be born in 1917, SERIOUSLY?
Would you rather be married off at age 13?
To a man who may be over 30?
Would you rather be pregnant at 15?

And yanked out of school as a teen,
And be told your full-time job hereafter
Is begetting male children for your lord and master?

What nonsense, what burnout?
Perspective you need, you silly child, be a sport
In this 21st century game of life and love
You're the lucky one, blessed from above!

Millions would want to be in YOUR PLACE
Obstacles big or small, be bold and face

Rising after every fall, every blow
Celebrate your feminine freedom, it's a superpower you know.

There is so much more to accomplish you see
So many girls that need to be set free
Women seen as impure because they menstruate
This is the 21st century, yes! Doesn't that make you irate?

Think of how FAR you have come
Yet, you have miles to go and then some
Think of the immense possibilities
With your healing powers come great responsibilities.

Why don't you use your privilege to do something?
Help Girls to think beyond anything
To be brave and to believe
Girls can do anything they mentally conceive!

Annamma concluded by saying-Learn everything you can
About this VAST universe
Miss not an opportunity to grow
Be ever curious
Find good friends, smile don't frown
Be that person that adjusts their crown.
Yes!!!
Be that doctor, healer, granddaughter, mother, other who proudly WEARS her crown.
Be that bold beautiful badass GODDESS who SHARES her crown
Wears her crown!
Shares her crown!!
Wears her crown!
Shares her crown!!

(My late grandmother is probably raising a toast to empowered women, something that she never had the chance to be in her lifetime.)
May our tribe increase!

(This section left blank for you, the reader, to write a tribute to a person who inspired and empowered you!)

Food, Feeding Tube, and Joy

(So many end up with feeding tubes they really didn't want in the first place, but had no advance directives to guide their children or medical providers).

Tears running down your eyes
You beat your chest
With every bit of strength
In your atrophied right arm.
You aim for that pacemaker
For that defibrillator
That looks like a sad anthill
Rising up in a shriveled thin chest.

You are completely paralyzed
In your left arm and leg
Even more atrophied
Than the rest of your body
You try so hard
To blow through your larynx
You huff and you heave
Out comes barely a squeak.

We offer you pen and paper
You grab it ....and toss it on
the floor
Every mitochondrion works
overtime.

You finally whisper NO
When the rehab nurse tries
For the fifth time
To give your clopidogrel
Thru' your feeding tube.

She and I hold your hand
Begging you to accept
Medicine- it's not your enemy

Let’s prevent another stroke, we say.
Out of nowhere
You find your barely audible
voice
“I don’t care” it says
More angry fierce tears follow.

We are so desperate
His daughter says
“It’s not your fault doc”
He refused medicine even before
the stroke
We are sad.
You continue to hit the
defibrillator
Angry that it’s working
Angry that you agreed to it.

The nurse sits on your low bed
I’m kneeling on the other side
We ask gently about your wishes
And that we will abide by.
The tears stop
You point vigorously to your
mouth and tongue
We ask if you want to eat
You nod and nod and nod…...

The speech pathologist
mysteriously appears,
And she starts to work with you.
You want real food right now
She promises she’ll try to get you
eating soon.

We ask about advance directives
You point to the defibrillator
And to your mouth

You want to keep the anthill, if
you can eat soon.

We ask about medicine
You smile in acceptance
You agree to comply……if only you
can eat again.
Food is joy!

A feeding tube can never replace
The palpable pleasure
Of taste, texture, touch.
You get your groove back
One eats to live
But one can also
……...Live to eat.

Flight to Paradise

(A rather young colleague passed away from metastatic hepatic cancer. She had not revealed her diagnosis even to close friends. I wrote this when I heard the shockingly sad news. Gazing silently at this flock made my heart lighter and filled me with hope for the morrow).

Hundreds take flight
Bidding goodbye to the setting sun
Evening has arrived
The day is coming to its natural end.

The birds know it
The bees know it
When it's time to say goodbye
It's time
To say farewell……

Not a thing
Can hold back the sun
The earth, from making
That slow rotation
In slow motion
So imperceptible that we go about our lives,
Without concern

Of the earth accelerating
Or decelerating.
Not a thing
Can hold back the human spirit
From taking that final flight
To a mystery destination.

The birds know it
As they fly their flock
To the land yonder

Fearlessly
Faithfully
Finally

The night will hold them
Like a grandmother's embrace,
In friendship
In comfort
In paradise
And dawn will come…….
Back with grace!

(This section is left blank for you, the reader, to write a tribute to a person who inspired and empowered you!)

Whispers of Color

(A short poem that flowed through random inspiration from a rainbow).

Must you take life for granted?
And so what if you do?
Will you dance faster
Sing louder
Paint more colors
Love too much
Live too slow?
Will you think yourself a coward for taking health for granted?

Because you were told all along
"Never take anything for granted"
Will your fate change
Will your fortune disappear
Will your ship never arrive
Or will it?
Because you had the audacity to take life for granted
For a moment…….

Because if you don't,
You live in the fear that it'll end
Too soon.
So, as surely as the sun rises after every sun set
As surely as the gravity that helps you stay grounded-
Take life for granted
A bit
And live life fully with the certainty that
as surely as the rainbow that follows

a cleansing rain
And whispers to you in color…….

"Live life
boldly,
brightly,
benevolently,
brilliantly!!"
……...You will land on your feet.

(Page left blank intentionally for you to write a few words on living life brightly!)

The Tumble That Makes Your Heart Rumble!

Much anticipation
People crowding
Eyes riveted to the spot
Not here yet
How much longer?

One by one they tumble
Like kids in a play gym
Thwack Thwack
Not a gentle sound

Whites, blacks, browns and pinks
A myriad of colors
Shapes
Unique sounds they make
The class is here
People trying to find the one
That makes their heart sing
"Oh, you're not lost
We don't need to file a claim
With ……. the airline"

The anticipation of the arrival
Of one's bag at the baggage carousel

Is almost as palpable
As a loving parent waiting
At the stop
For her tiny offspring
To tumble out of the school bus!

(Written as I awaited arrival of two checked-in suitcases at the airport baggage claim - the first bag tumbled out FIRST……...the second arrived LAST after the 108th bag).

Chapter 2:
The Shape of the World

The Star in the Sky

January 1st at 7:29 AM is when the sun chose to rise
A wintry New Year's Day, a Sunny surprise
Blazing bright hues lit up the sky
Even as most stars said good night and goodbye.

Our planet began another turn around the brightest star
The SUN sent rays to touch near and far
Trees looked bored with skinny skeletons bared
The hibernating grass was sad, brown and withered.

Yet, no matter the season, the Sun rises
It's chilly outside, I want to stay in bed,
But the sun still rises
There is a sheet of ice on the lake, sunrise will happen
There are no ducks in the pond, sunrise will not slacken.

The sun never takes a day off.
Never a vacation! Never a handoff
Always "on call" with no coverage pod
No "son" or daughter to provide
On- call coverage to
 the "Sun" God
(from professional duties.)

The Sunny Sun is showing no burn-out,
Despite burning all day, respite without.......

It may be a cloudy, gloomy, rainy day
Yet he is out with no delay
The sun must be a child- he plays hide and seek
Between clouds and raindrops, he takes a peek.

Mere mortals need vacations galore
The sun works all year without keeping score
Are you ready (already) to take your next vacation?
Beware, the "vacation-less" Star will follow you to that
Sunny destination.

Happy new year!

Grey Cloud, Silver Lining

(There's something so mystical about being suspended in midair and yet we take the ride for granted at times, in the midst of chaos of TSA checks, crowded sitting areas, and lost baggage in airports).

The tip of my metal wing
Is inspired to soundlessly sing
As it barely touches your ray
As if to say Hello! And pray.

I fly over the Andes range
Not for a moment do I feel strange
Mountains strong and mysterious
Deep craters and snowcapped peaks, so ponderous.

Your rays meet absolutely no cloud
The azure CIELO is sans sound
The hum of my engine penetrating space
Draws zero attention from the chilly -13° embrace!

Not a bird……. except me of course
Metallic body, gray and morose
Inside me is a cabin full of vibrant lives
Children, parents, husbands and wives.

You are shining so bright today
Have you come out to vigorously play?
With mountain crevices that wish to hide
You seek them out…...found you! Time to unhide.

I bask in your beauty as I fly
Sunshine so gloriously Blue and Bly
Your rays turn my grey metal skin into silver shining
Yes! Even a grey airplane has a silver lining.

Cloudy Story

Clouds tell stories
Stories of love
When they hover over
A mother holding her newborn
A baby gazing at its father
Newlyweds kissing at an outdoor altar
A first-time grandparent
A kitty rubbing her face
On the human she adores!

Stories of tragedy
When the body of a child
Is washed onto a beach
Drowned when parents fleeing
A war-torn region
Jump on to a boat with a thousand refugees
Stories of hatred
When nations fight
Eighteen-year-olds go to war
Not knowing

Why they're killing
Who they're killing
When they're killing
Where they're killing
What they're killing

Stories of friendship
When they look down and see
A picnic in a park
A picque-nicque with laughter
Glasses clinking, People drinking
Cold sodas, and hot coffee
Munching on fried chicken, deviled eggs,
Sandwiches, crackers
Indulging a sweet tooth with cupcakes

Stories and more stories

Of a president being inaugurated
Of a lifeless body being
Thrown into a mass grave
Of a child squealing with the joy
Of jumping higher on a trampoline
Of polluting factories spewing smoke
That rises up to pollute
My pristine cloudy fluffiness.

Of sorrows and joy
Of pain and pleasure
Of mystery and lucidity
Of the rational and irrational
Of the sensible and the senseless
Of the mundane and the extraordinary
And all things in between…….
I gaze upon humanity
And await more stories!

The Shenandoah Show

A riot of joyous color
No room for sickly pallor
A perfectly aligned yellow divider
Wishes to blend in with the leafy cover.
Shapely Shadows in play
On the gray tar all day
As the trees tell a story
Whispered in rustling glory ……
Are they saying good night
To autumn's fading light?
Anticipating the winter
Leaves getting scarcer……
The rally before the storm
One last hurrah, as they form
A rain shower of beautiful leaves
In reds, yellows, browns and greens
Mother Nature's riotous showy ceremony
Deserving an Oscar or a Tony!

The Goddess of Liberty

Barefooted pursuit of liberty and joy
The statue of liberty
Standing tall, sublime, and majestic
Bearing witness to the poor, the fatigued
The huddled masses yearning
To live, to breathe, to be free.

You, are the symbol of freedom, of compassion
A goddess who's shattered her shackles
Nothing holds you back. As you welcome
Immigrants broken by the burden of living.

Does your monochromatic sculpted sea green body
Long to be free of its coppery inertness?
And feel alive, be happy, show emotion like a free woman?
To unbind your hidden feet, to play a game of soccer?

To do something that nobody expects from you,
To reincarnate as a vibrant Indian woman
To wear a saree, a radiant bindi on your forehead
A nose ring, bangles jingling on your wrists.

To shed your blue-green patina
To cover yourself in the vitality of red, yellow and purple
To be free of constricting shoes
To feel the dirt with barefooted toes
To kick that ball high, out of the park.

Oh Lady Liberty, carry that torch higher
To liberate every tortured soul
To feel unfettered innocent childlike freedom
To smile the unrestrained smile of playful surrender
And inspire our right to-

Life, liberty and the pursuit of joy!

Mermaid in Cancun

The naughty ocean!
Dramatic is the purple sky above
Clouds painting artful expressions......she watches from a
Cove
Distant thunderstorms looming galore
Threatening to fill the brimming ocean some more.

Passing dark clouds in purple fury
A pounding deluge unleashing its glory
Yet, unperturbed is the ocean shore
Watches this "mermaid with feet"- she's hidden in the
Cove.

Playful little waves dance in glee
They approach her toes, then laughingly flee
Retreating quickly, then rushing forward
Like a child playing "catch me if you can"
While running backward.

Ferocious creatures-they can deliver a fright
As big as a wall of water can a wave take flight
A tsunami can bring skyscrapers under
The power of water is stronger than thunder.

Walking at the edge of warm water
Waves big and small drawing feet under
Enveloping each ankle in gentle embrace
Kissing each toe with childlike grace.

This human mermaid wants a tail-
NOT feet
The underwater Mer-folks she wants to meet
Be rocked by the ocean wind and brine
With her face glowing in the brightest Sunshine ......

The fairytale of the little mermaid
Longing for human feet is NOT sad
Longing for something one cannot have easily
Is a story, old as mankind and will continue perpetually.

The next time you walk on pearly white wet sand, beach
That feels like soft pillows, so grand
Feel the music of water, wind ……hear it
As you become one with Mother Nature's kindred spirit!

And then you leave, not wanting to return to reality
Saying goodbye to the playful ocean waves, so naughty
Hoping to come back for one more game,
    Of "Catch me if you can" -
    Oh, to be a child again.

Porange

The sky is brilliant
It cannot decide on an accent
Should it stay pink or orange?
Maybe a compromise, PORANGE!
Winter is not quite over
And sunshine doesn't last forever
Yet, the sun sets in joyful glory
Tomorrow to rise, to begin a brand-new story.

A Cocktail of Colors

(When events beyond our control, shape our world in a way that seem unreasonable or unrecognizable, nature can give us solace. I wrote this on a pensive note pondering the future of the young and the not so young. And feeling comforted that resilience is integral to the human condition and reflected in nature every single day.
The best part about having a long work drive is the knowing that observing nature around the confines of a vehicle brings clarity to the mind. Nature seems to stay more constant than the fickleness of mere mortal creatures and will not disappoint with revealing her beauty, come dawn or dusk! Nature reflects one's self-healing and vice versa)

The SKY is Intense!
I drive to work on a road so quiet except for the hum of engines
As dawn cracks open a clearing in the clouds.
Like a volcano on a rampage spewing energetic lava
and painting the sky with fire

Emerges the Sun Goddess in her finery
On a chariot of clouds taking on an iridescent aura.
Reflecting the radiant red rays
of a rising sun
or

could this be the setting sun?

Could I be driving back from work and facing the Goddess in the opposite direction?
Life at both ends of the spectrum
can look alike for some.

A baby with many days ahead
An elder with her days ending

Helpless maybe.
Hopeless never.
The sun sets……only to rise again.

RESILIENCE - a sure manifestation
of the shimmering sunshine inside of us……...
It might dim, only to brighten again

Like a dormant volcano
that brings forth a flame of fiery fury.
Like red traffic lights that turn green
When the time is ripe.

Chapter 3: Ordinary Magic

The Kit-Kat Santa

(My daughter's orange tabby is a hilarious little fellow who makes his human buddies smile and smile some more!)

Cheddar is his given name
Naughty and Nice gives him fame
Most times he's wholesome as cheese and cracker
Except when he's raiding the food bag - our little pantry hacker!

One moment you're cuddling this baby bear
The very next, he's scrambling like a monkey without care
He wants his head patted like a puppy
While his mouth opens roundly like a fishy guppy!

He tries to do Yoga poses like a human
While humans hold cat-poses with acumen……
Paradoxical is this quirky world
Everything's compared to something else-so weird.

Cheddar is back to being a cat
He's our Kitty Katty kit-kat
He once attempted to take the MCAT
The exam was too easy; he fell asleep on the doormat!

He can do a free PET-SCAN
In under a minute's span,
Sniff you from toe to top
A CAT- scan, no problem……stop at Cheddar's discount shop!

He is now taking a break from being a baby, a monkey, a PET & CAT-scanner, a puppy
A bear, a human, a cracker, a hacker and a guppy;
In my dream, he drank a big bottle of Fanta,
And transformed into an orange Santa!!

Anita's Artwork

If the SPEED of light
Were to transform its might
Into an artist's brush
Working in a soundless hush
Renouncing a straight line
Instead zigzagging thru cloud nine
To ruffle the universe
Embodying a poetesses' verse
And land on a 9 x 12-inch canvas
Encoding deep emotions in the hippocampus
Would the SPEED of lightning
Masquerade as your vibrant painting??

Monkey Baby

He peeks through the banisters
A little shy
A little curious
He descends the stairs

Like a prince so regal
With his orange cape
His ears pointy
Like a perky little crown

Our baby boy
Ever such a rascal
Turning faucets on
Letting water drip
Turning the sink into
A tiny swimming pool

Opening shelves
Hiding in cabinets
Cooing and babbling

A growing baby boy
We named you CHEDDAR

If you were a pizza
We would call you Cheddar-Roni
If you were a Christmas conifer
We would call you Cheddafer

Sometimes you behave like
A little terrorist
Terrorizing your big sister

And encroaching upon her territory
We call you the Cheddarist

Burrowing inside our recyclable flag bag
At times you are a patriot
Our Cheddariot
When you're cute as orange pumpkins
We call you Cheddikins

A rose by any other name would smell just as sweet.
A kitty by any name would be just as kittenish

And our little monkey Cheddar by any other name
would be
just as
"Cheddarish"!

Coffee

The sights, the smells and the taste of love
Some people cannot do without this feeling
That craving engulfs their entire being
Morning, afternoon or twilight
Their world revolves around this ultimate delight.

The sight, the aroma is glorious
Without it they are furious
The taste is a potent stimulant
The joy it brings them is magnificent.

So why is it called brain juice?
Because thru' your veins it will sluice
Pumping like high octane
Liquid energy to ease all pain.

Many call it a cup of Joe
But why not call it a cup of Beau?
Or rename it to a cup of Jane
Why not a cup of Shane, Elaine or Lorraine?

Well, many an unhappy story abound
Navy secretary Josephus Daniels around
In the navy, alcohol prohibited and coffee substituted
Sailors renamed it Cup of Josephus, a cupful of sarcasm
unlimited.

Some folks named it JAMOKE
A cuppa Java and Mocha bespoke
Java in Indonesia and Mocha a city in Yemen
They grow beans that put you in coffee heaven.

To some, coffee is the sweetest perfume
The language of eternal Love and Lume

Pulling each into its rich dark embrace
Like a lover with a smiling face.

A French press, Bialetti or a latte
From Arabica to Robusta, bitter or dolce
Expresso, cappuccino, ristretto, Lungo or Americano
Cortado, Doppio, Affogato, Mocha or Macchiato.

Concentrated coffee with hot water- espresso
Espresso shot with steamed milk and foam - cappuccino
Espresso shot with just foam - macchiato
2 shots of espresso- Doppio.

Coffee with chocolate – mocha
Short pulled espresso- ristretto
Long pulled espresso. – Lungo
Coffee with ice cream – Affogato

Are you adequately confused by this coffee terminology train?
Well, have a simple americano to clear your brain!

Caffeine lover or Caffeinated lover
Fiercely bonded duo,
inseparable power.

Aisle Seat Nightmare

As they pack in people like many a sardine
In a tin-can-like airplane cabin
I wait with bated breath
Even though it's not a matter of life and death
To see who's going to occupy the seat in the middle
Between me and the window seat, a riddle
Is it going to be a man, woman or child?
Someone that snores or someone mild?
Someone that breathes with a wheeze
Someone whose cough sounds like a sneeze?
Someone that drinks 3 cups of coffee
And juice since it's free
And climbs over my aching legs all flight long
Steps on my poor toes like King-Kong
As toilet stops they make
Every thirty minutes, a bathroom break
I hope and pray to fare better
Such that every aisle seat passenger's nightmare
ain't bitter!

Bellary and Krish

I was a little girl living in Bellary
Who started writing a story
On a littler boy called Krish
Who had many a wish
He meandered on and on
From town to town
From street to street
Until he was beat……
Fifty pages later
It didn’t get any better
It still didn’t have a plot
Or an anchoring slot
The boy kept wandering
And I kept wondering
He must’ve walked around the globe
And outgrown his wardrobe.

The White Coat Fashionista

She dissects the word fashion
It's a noun, it's also a verb with action
"To make something, a popular trend"
A clothing and cosmetics style newness to ascend.

She uses her diagnostic skill
To critically evaluate skin and nails and hair with thrill
What's the etiology of that pimple?
And where hath disappeared my dimple?
And what is the pathology of that wrinkle?
The collagen is in free falling dwindle
Objectively, I might be over the hill
Subjectively I am forever 21 maybe 31 still.

What is the physiology of curly hair?
Oval hair follicles, uneven keratin, a deadly genetic pair
Round follicles and even keratin make hair straight
Disulfide bonds can be broken to undo a trait.
Now let's get to the biochemistry section
Hyaluronic acid, vitamin C, niacinamide in
Every beauty potion
Retinol is a must for youthful skin?
Chemical or mineral- use your choice of sunscreen.

Let's get to the psychology of fashion
Why do some embrace the passion?
Of styles and trend
Human emotions, values, insecurities and identities blend.
Hey, some peer pressure adds to the fun
Affix a Birkin bag to your look and stun
Color and creativity to make your inner artist proud
Fashion is like sunshine glamorizing a cloud
Gosh, a cloud would look so dull without sun and shine
A touch of fashion does make one look fine!

Why is Poetry Necessary?

To TRANSFORM mundane words into something meaningful.

To TRANSFER thoughts in your head to a verbal or written medium in the most creative manner.

To TRANSITION what's felt in the heart to your soul in the most heartfelt and soulful way possible.

To TELEPORT oneself instantaneously from the earth to the constellation of stars, to the Milky Way galaxy and beyond.

To TALK about "waiting" like a flower that blooms slowly, softly, silently, without compromising its beauty.

To TRANSPORT one's imaginative ideas onto a visible object with rhyme, reason and rhythm.

To TELL the world that we are more than just words and phrases and symbols and deeds, but that the sum of those can make our hearts hum, our minds meander, our bodies breathe and our souls sing!

To TRANSFORM the depths of our being that can go unsaid to a visible emotion that speaks truth and vulnerability for the world to see, hear and feel.

To TRANSCEND the darkness of our inner and outer lives and blossom into the universe of
hope and joy!

And to TRANSPLANT sickness with healing-

Poetry is the best medicine to soothe the hurts hurled by the world

And

Be

the better version of yourself.

(This was written as I read through tens of poems as a first-time judge for a Poetry Society of Texas contest. A priceless experience! Add your own reasons as to why you read poetry and prose and fiction and nonfiction? What does it mean and why does it matter to you?)

Chapter 4: Weight, We Carry

The Horizon's Gentle Embrace

Her nostrils flared, and her eyes were ablaze.
"It's so unfair," she said, "that the stars did not align
for my poor mother, barely 37,
who can see her end approaching."

A single tear, like a crystal bead,
slid down her beautiful bronze cheek
clouding her gaze.

"Death, don't you dare darken my doorstep,"
she said furiously…….
A deep flush rose as she turned to me,
her mother's hospice physician.

"I think I know what's to come - do not gloss over the inevitable, doc.
Is my mother soon headed six feet underground?"
"I've prayed over this, but there's no Hail Mary……. I know.
It's the headlong pace of her decline, that's making me feel out of joint,
and the meager information from the hospital
what do I do next? How do I cope without mom?"
She cries in anguish.

"Every day, Mother seems to melt another notch.
Her beautiful eyes look opaque."

I perceive the depth of sorrow that's plotting against this 17-year-old.
Grief stings her heart like the piercing point of a needle,
leaving her prone to a wound so deep.

I prop open the door, pointing to the sunset,
asking her to imagine a boat at the rim,
sailing gently, without worry of infinite roam or scope.

A stroke of fading sunlight
makes the boat feel swept into an ocean of warmth,
of love.

She imagines her mother unbound, unwound, unwavering,
weighted not by her terminal illness anymore-
from nadir to zenith
sailing into the horizon's gentle embrace.

Fear

I wake up at 5am
Drenched in sweat
Is it hot flashes?
Or is it fear?
What is fear?
Why do I fear, fear?
Why is it so omnipresent?
Where does it come from and go to?
Babies feel fear
Old people do as well.
Is it more in the old
Versus the young?
Animals feel fear
Do plants feel any?
How would we know anyways?
Unless they scream and holler?
Why does it make armpits wet?
The heart beat helter-skelter?
The bladder and bowels
Feel uneasy and at risk?
We take precautions
We take extra care
To prevent that unwelcome feeling
To drive it far far away.
We pray to the gods
And Goddesses too......
The world is full of deities
Humans need the comfort, so!
And yes, we do feel comforted
By the myriad prayers
Chanting and meditation
A non-prescription antidote for fear......

Buffalo Hump and Moon Face

Delicate darling they called her
She wheezed and coughed
On the playground not knowing

Why she could not keep up with her peers……
They hopped and jumped merrily on the playground

She sat alone on the elementary school bench

She was a preemie,
Had a lot of catching up to do……
She stayed rather small

Short of breath while playing a game of hopscotch
Wheezing trying to jump rope
She had childhood asthma they said……

No inhalers available no nebulizer treatments
All they had was this horrible bitter medicine called Tedral.

Her grandmother pinched her nose
Stuck a spoonful of medicine down her throat…….
Followed by a salty pickle

Then a gulp of fresh air to make it go down

Don't you dare vomit they warned,
We will do it again and again and ………
The medicine is keeping you alive
Bitter will make you better

Decades have passed
The taste of bitterness will forever linger……
Steroids came along
She was pumped with powdered steroids
A homeopathic Doctor promised a powdered cure

A moon face and buffalo hump followed.........

A lifetime of osteoporosis and myopathy
The girl could not jump or skip or hop
But she breathed and stayed alive.

Delicate darling she was jeered until the words rang sweet.......
Something "delicate" is fine and beautiful.
Somebody's "darling" is what most people seek to be.

But how hurtfully taunting

when those two words are put together?!

Mind, Body, and Heat

(Initially published in Collin college's FORCES magazine in 2025)

A smoldering ember
Right in the junction of my sternum and abdomen
Lights up like flashes
Sometimes accompanied
By audiovisual effects
Screeching like the sirens
Of an ambulance
Trying to make its way
Thru rush hour traffic

The sirens building in crescendo
Pushing aside every vehicle in sight.
This ember exudes power
It controls me
Every organ
Exposed to this sizzling fury

Is this the hell fire
That I was warned about
When I was just a little kid
Who refused to obey every rule set by an adult?

I feel like the ember inside
Makes me perspire
So profusely
That I'm in a bowl of scalding soup
That is bubbling
Like a witch's cauldron

But turns into an ice bath
In the next 30 seconds.
Fever and chills
Dryness in one place
Overflowing moisture in another

Melting bones getting softer
Arteries and veins getting harder
Could it all be happening
In the same body
How's this dichotomy even possible?

Everything is going downhill
Or ......is it?
My brain still works
Those moods swing back and forth
Like a swing torn in a hurricane
Landing on a spot of humor....

I can still tease myself
Even when sitting in a bubbling hot tub full of sweat
Am I experiencing the glorious Texas summer?

The exciting triple digits that apparently can cook an egg on a sidewalk?
Oh no!
These are just exciting hot flashes
That bubble like the molten lava from a volcano

Oh no! Menopause

The pause my patients warned me about
The pause that men rarely have pleasure of experiencing.
The pause I wish to fast forward,
The pause that's taught me patience
The pause that's made me more empathic with my patients
The pause in middle life that makes a woman realize that hot flashes and Texas summers are long lasting, but temporary

Even this heat shall pass.......

Soul

Born out of my mind
Married to my body
Not sure where you reside.
Are you my inner child?
Do you rest within my heart
Then migrate to my brain?
Do you seek a better organ
When my brain has headaches,
Or when my stomach dares my heart
To a duel of heartburn?
Are you my invisible consciousness
My conscience?
Do you carry a gender?
Were you a little girl
When I played house with dolls?
A little boy
When I was called a tomboy
For climbing trees?
Are you the miracle
That saves me from myself?
I hear you'll divorce my body
And move on when I am gone.
We are not eternal lovers,
You and me
Bound to live and die together…
I guess not?

Darwin's theory doesn't apply.
Natural selection, struggle for existence
Survival of the fittest –
None apply.
You endure beyond the worldly.
You are the indivisible
The irreducible
The microcosm in the macrocosm
The Universe within the Multiverse.
So, I'm glad that you - my SOUL
Will live on
In life
and
Beyond death.

A Deathly Dilemma

Who was the Indian author from my middle school
Kannada language class
that said-
"Why does life put sweet jaggery in one person's mouth
while it puts bitter neem leaves in somebody else's?
Why do some people sail through life with nary a mishap
while others are fraught with tension?"

A cousin's wife lays dying
On a ventilator that does all the work of breathing.

The palliative Nurse Practitioner
Approaches gingerly
Wondering if we are
Another family that's going to resist nature
And ask for a dead brain to be resuscitated.

She's had a massive stroke
At age 49
Her pupils are dilated
She has no brain reflexes
She failed the apnea test
She has normal vital signs though
She could go on and on
On the ventilator.

There's nothing wrong with her
From the neck down
The practitioner says you can take your time.
No, my cousin is brave
He says "I know she's already dead, what's the point in
keeping her heart alive when her brain is gone?"

The Nurse Practitioner heaves an invisible sigh
I know she's young she says sadly
Faintly in a voice of concession
And consolation.

Like I've done many a time
When I come across a reasonable family
That doesn't ask for the impossible.

For me to keep a 90-year-old
With advanced dementia
Alive with a feeding tube
To rehabilitate their 85-year-old spouse
With terminal cancer
Such that he can have
One more round of the horrible chemotherapy
That's made him so miserable.
I remember my mentor from decades ago saying-
Don't keep flogging that dying horse, it'll do no good.
And yet that's exactly
What many expect of me. I fail them……

My cousin is exceptionally strong
He sits numbly with tears flowing
Down his cheeks
We talk a bit. We stop
Immersed in deep thought

Of life and death
She was fine at dinner yesterday
Just went downstairs
To eat a snack before bedtime
And never returned
This happened in a minute

Alive one moment
And gone the next

Does life leave a body so quickly?

He says in wonderment over and again.
She never made any advance directives
But she was diabetic
Don’t think she’s a good organ donor
We talk about how we cannot take our organs to heaven
Why not give them to those
That might need
A heart, a kidney, a pancreas, a lung
A cornea, some skin…….

I am such a bad husband
I knew she was eating fast food
I should’ve stopped her
I was reminding her to take medicines and exercise
I made her so mad
She told me I was treating her like a child
But what do you do when someone you love
behaves like a child?
How do you not treat them like a child?
I could not pull the food out of her mouth
Maybe I should have tried
I’m going to live with regrets
He says sadly with a fresh burst of sadness
I try to console him………

The Embrace of the White Coat

Why do physicians wear white coats?
Why not purple, or red, or yellow, or black coats?
When I don the white,
a sense of responsibility settles
and my demeanor changes
like a sudden hush in a thunderstorm.
I'm less playful
more thoughtful
the coat whispers "you have much to do."
My shoulders feel the weight
of the trust from a sick person given like a gift
a heavy precious boulder.
I see every stain- visible and invisible
on the pristine white,
marks from patients who've suffered
with medical problems,
with treatment of medical problems,
without treatment of medical problems,
with adverse effects of medication
too little, too much, or just right.
Each stain faint,
like a fault only I can see in the darkness.
Ghost of an unforgettable moment
shimmering on fabric

like pale moonlight on rippling waves.
And yet, my white coat feels like an embrace
a loving arm around me from an old, long-lost friend
who wishes nothing but the purity of her own heart
rendering strength in the firmest terms
lifting my sagging spirits
and crowning me with the objectivity necessary
to bring comfort
to another human soul.
Untainted, untouched, white.
The Hippocratic oath that I wear on my skin!

(Page left blank intentionally for you to write a few thoughts on your ordinary and extraordinary musing!)

Chapter 5: In Celebration

A Golden Birthday

(A Golden Birthday Poem for a dear friend)

Hush oh hush, rumor has it
Her cake and candles are lit
That golden birthday, a milestone to aspire
Blow 50 candles quick, lest your cake catch on fire!

That birth certificate must be fake
Manipulated by an envious drake
There's just no way you could be Five-0
They surreptitiously doubled your age, we know.

Were you ever told, just act your age?
Or, age is just a number on a page
And that fifty is the new thirty
Believe them not, it's just time for a lively party.

Failing eyesight may call for
3-dioptre glasses
Taste buds cannot tell pickles from molasses
Joint crepitus, scalp pruritus, flatus and tinnitus
Everything's falling apart, oh this traitorous apparatus!

Fear not, some body parts still work
Like the brachioradialis reflex and patellar jerk
Menopause may put sweat glands in overdrive
Hot flashes push you into the pool with a swan dive.

You may have hit a half century
And conquered the distance from Mars to Mercury
But you'll be forever, to your friends and family
A child, sibling, spouse, parent, buddy, never an anomaly.

Middle age is fast arriving
Broad mind and narrow waist, places exchanging
Deadline to blame parents for all problems is expiring
It's not a cloud, but your hair that has the silver lining.

Stones you begin to collect like gold
Gall and kidney and bladder stones, behold
Eat extra fruit and veggies- more tomato in your Bloody Mary
Cucumber gin martini, or bourbon at dinner with cherry!

Jokes aside, aging has its perks
Hidden talent, time to safely unleash your quirks
You can shrug off comments, savor the compliments
And blame everything else on "senior moments."

A marathon you have run
Biking and hiking under the sun
Warrior sculpt and yoga get you excited
Your fitness commitment is genuine and unrestrained.

A loving daughter, a supportive wife
Two lovely teenagers you're raising without strife
Your gentle honesty is a virtue
Humility and unpretentiousness are you!

Adjectives flow from your friends galore
Your elegance, enthusiasm, authenticity they adore
Sincerity, determination, honesty and confidence
Thoughtfulness, friendliness, inclusiveness and persistence.

Bubbly, positive, poised, approachable and stylish
Well rounded, pleasant, innocent but never childish
Everyone admires your smiling demeanor
And wishes you well in every fabulous endeavor.

How far you have come, isn't it amazing?
How much you have grown, and keep on growing
Mind, body and soul with wisdom overflowing
Each experience totally worth sharing.

Social distance, mask, the corona world notwithstanding
Our heartfelt hope is just as loving
Much happiness we wish foremost
To your grand journey,
We raise a "virtual" Pop Fizz Clink champagne toast!!

Paro

(In honor of a brilliant friend who's an infectious disease specialist by day and a writer, a RJ for a local radio station and a teacher of English writing by night).

Our lovely Paro aka Parul
When is she not cheerful?
Her name means “Graceful”
Sanskrit for beautiful.

The power of Goddess Parvati
Gifts from Goddess Saraswati
She writes with such charm
Her presence makes us feel fuzzy and warm.

Be it a jockey on the radio
Or a mover & shaker in the studio
She can party like a rockstar
For everyone, she has raised the bar.

An affectionate mommy of three
Not a moment she has free
Doctor, dancer, choreographer, Bollywood lover
Mimicry artist, superwoman and total charmer.

Accomplishments she has to the moon and back
Into everything, power she can pack
But most importantly she has no airs, no pretend
One of a kind, she’s truly a joyful friend!

In Honor of a Super Dynamic Surgeon Friend

What do you call a mind
That's so unique and hard to find?
It's brilliant and bright
It sparkles like stars in the night!

This unique mind powers a person
Who is endearingly full of passion
Be it climate change or gun reform
No serious topic is off limits to this thoughtful mom.

Said Florence Nightingale, in a voice very clear-
"How very little can be done, if under the spirit of fear?"
More Docs like my friend we need, who are fearless
Talk the talk, but walk the walk nonetheless.

She is a dynamo par excellence
True fire is her core essence
She's thoughtful, she's kind, she's "one of a kind"
Insightful wisdom regularly floods her mind.

Politicians without spine, be aware
She's coming for your scalp and hair
Doesn't matter if you're blue or red, or on either coast
If you don't perform, you're toast.

She's a loving daughter, a faithful partner
A very affectionate mom to a son and daughter
How does she juggle home and operating table?
With her invisible superwoman cape and sharp scalpel!

Now, this CMO,
Is modest……so we hear about it
6 months into June-O!
She is CHIEF since Jan 2024,
We celebrated proudly the week before.

Too many chiefs and not enough Indians
A phrase that rankled native Indians and Indo-Americans
Friend- you'll beat the irony off its face
Chief and Indian-woman, a role you'll ace!

Our hearts for you swell with pride
We feel the joy of a brand-new bride
Even as you ace the doctor-admin combo
We will never forget you're first and foremost, a dynamo!!

A God (or Goddess) a Day!

(Context: My devout medical school classmate who lives in Bangalore has archived his dad's huge collection of pictures of Indian Gods and Goddesses on google drive and begins his morning by posting one a day on WhatsApp!)

'A blessing a day'
He starts his day
By sending a picture of a God or goddess
From his archives in Google documents
Without missing a day.

Every single morning, his time
To correspond with my evening
For years without fail
A comforting routine.

IST AND CST
Time zones across the globe
Seem to merge in a blessing
Of peace!

Every day is a surprise
There never seems to be a repeat
Of pictures of a god
Be it Shiva, Vishnu, one of the avatars.

Goddesses galore
Resplendent in their Alankara
Parvati, Lakshmi, Saraswathi
The eternal trio of protection, prosperity, perspicacity!

It must brighten his morning
To awaken the world
With a connection to divinity
A mantra!

A Dynamic Explorer

(On an adventure loving friend who loves to run, hike, climb, swim with sharks, travel to the Himalayas……)

There was the Commanding Mr. Columbus
Sailed seven seas without fuss
And the Valorous
Mr. Vasco da Gama
Discovered land with panorama!

And then there's our modern-day explorer
Who's as brave as Columbus aka Christopher
The quest for yet another adventurous zone
Deeply embedded in her sinew and bone.

Every day, new hills she's hiking
When she's not running
And when she's not running or hiking
You'll find her ocean diving.

Hawaii - Stairway to heaven
She traveled up a treacherous mountain
Using sharp spikes on shoes
Trudging up and down with nary a bruise.

Machu Picchu was a breeze
High altitude, no problem, not a wheeze
Egypt to Peru, traveler par excellence
Undoubtedly, and a Marathoner of eminence.

Everest base camp and scaling Pikes Peak
Weathering a Patagonian windstorm as we speak.

Real estate maven, doctor
Retirement early adopter
F.I.R.E, she epitomized at forty
Unbridled adventurer, super sporty.

Her spirituality is running
Her meditation is hiking
She is a Yogini who has fun
Mostly she's "poetry" in motion!

(Page left blank for you to write about an adventurous person.)

Unified Dynamos

(I'm part of a huge tribe of desi women physicians called "The Dynamo Docs". Wrote this poem in honor of the members in 2022 when the messaging app-WhatsApp increased the limit from the 200's to 1024 members or so).

Our dynamic tribe is multiplying
30 new member entries in 30 minutes in June 2022 were staggering
750 plus merry sailors rowing upstream
Makes for a much happier dream!

A family with talents abundant
Singers, dancers, painters and knitters exuberant
Runners, wunners, swunners
Also, slow walkers and talkers!

Our active dynamo sub-groups number, how many?
Dynamo Fitness
Dynamo Artisans
Dynamo Explorers
FIRE dynamos
Dynamo dancing queens
Dynamo retirement
Dynamo sizzlers
Dynamo nutrition
Dynamo fashion frenzy
Have I left out any?
Some of us require gentle reactivating
Eg): Dynamo intermittent fasting
Fasters- Let's get back into our groove
Our busy bodies, we need to improve
Retired groups can "un" retire
Hey Dynamo Sizzlers, we need some fire!

Fasting followed by feeding
Our poor tummies cannot suffer
Yummy food is life's best buffer.

The Dynamo Retreat will get bigger
Into a ranch, we will fit no longer
For the forthcoming 2030 Antarctica trip
Gosh, we will need a giant cruise ship.

Dr. M, our energetic brilliant and cool founder
Brought us all nicely together
Her motto: Let's learn from each other and grow
As we navigate days, some fast, some slow.

Dr. K, guru of fitness honors
She converted non-runners into marathoners
Dynamo fitness transformed some couch potatoes
Into toned and terrific tornadoes!

There are group rules: do's and don'ts,
The do's: Participate! Don't be the won'ts,
Religion and politics, we discuss with care
Respect and humility are a must, as thoughts we share.

So, as we strengthen this sisterhood
Stand by each other through bad and good
Let's play with each other joyously
Voila! Let's be one big happy WhatsApp family!

The Modern GREEN Santa

Dashing thru' the snow
In his Tesla inspired sleigh
O'er the fields we go
Regenerating energy all the way!
Bells with hybrid ring'
Making battery power bright
What fun it is to ride and sing
An EV song tonight.
Jingle bells, jingle bells,
Economy all the way.
Oh! what fun it is to ride
In a carbon footprint reducing sleigh.

Jingle bells, jingle bells
Jingle all the way
Oh! what fun it is to ride
In a battery powered open sleigh
The modern Santa Claus
Has laid off reindeer and horse
So, Rudolph and his red nose
Are looking for a job.
If Uber is hiring reindeer
Please give Rudolph a call
He'll jingle the horn of an EV car
And drive you near or far.
Jingle bells, jingle bells,
Jingle all the way;
Oh! what fun it is to ride
In Santa's plug-in electric sleigh!
(Happy Christmas to all of you. Whether you've been naughty or nice, Santa will hopefully bring y'all presents in his EV sleigh!)

Suppi's Splendor

(In honor of my very inspiring neurologist friend Supriya who performed her dance debut called Arangetram in her fourth decade of life and subsequently has participated in numerous beauty pageants recently winning the Mrs. Universe runner up crown.)

The play of transcendental light and sound
Melodies competing soft and loud
Percussion, strings and wind instrument
The vocalist - each an integral part of an ornament.

Gods and Goddesses come to eternal life
As the dancer depicts joy and strife
Slaying demons, drawing sword and blood
Elegant Mudras, abhinaya pouring into a passionate flood.

Sensuous Satyabhama one moment
Dangerous Durgadevi killing her wicked opponent
Ananda Tandava is sheer Splendor
Comes forth the Trinity- creator, preserver and destroyer!

Exquisite is each pose
Hard to describe in poetry or prose
So strong yet delicate is this Apsara
Is she a stunning sculpture…... or a twinkling Tara!?

From doctor to the Mrs. Universe stage
SuppiShine- you're a delightful Texas classic rage
Takes utmost diligence to excel in things extracurricular
Of course, you're winner of Mrs. Worldwide Popular!

Neurologist by day, many a fulfilling role you play
Mom, wife, daughter, runner, biker, TikToker, Model on runway
Unwavering dedication to science and art
Your awe-inspiring journey is led by brain and heart!

When Life Was Simple

Childhood is like no other hood
It's the time when life feels good
When time feels endless
And space is filled with innocence-
so boundless.
Why should childhood end at age 9 or 12 or 15?
At twenty or fifty or ninety!
It's not an age written in concreted land
Boundaries appear and disappear in sand
Feeling childlike curiosity and wonder
The ability to guiltlessly ponder
Friendship and joy experienced sans rift
That is an ageless forever gift!

Friendship and Water

Friendship is like a moody ship
In this ocean of life that feels like a nautical blip
Sailing smoothly when the waters are calm
Like a comforting warm breezy balm
On a wild ride when waters turn choppy
Friendship can sink or get sloppy
Some will die
Others survive
Nurturing it is more than a frivolous pastime
The ones that survive could sail a precious lifetime.

Friendship on Stovetop

(You'd likely have to cook Indian food- Golden yellow Daal and Fluffy White Basmati Rice- to make sense of this poem)

A symphony of aromas
Surround my heart
The sound of mustard seeds
Spluttering merrily like giddy little school kids
Dancing in puddles
Oblivious to the heat
As coconut oil wraps each seed coating it
Smoothly.

In jump the Cumin, the Curry leaves, the Chilli pods, the Garlic
Merry as friends meeting after years
Flavors blending like friendship
Inseparably.

The friends in the mixture are restless
As they join the sea of yellow.
Wondering if the golden lentils will ever accept them
Will they be separated
Friendless and lonely
Like tiny fish in a big pond?

Soon they find themselves
Tossed on white fluffy soft basmati
As they make their way
Into a cavity called the mouth.
They find themselves pushed and pulled

This way and that way
Until they are all ONE with each other
A fine mush of togetherness
Unafraid of separation.
Their destiny in one place

As they hear exclamations of contentment
Joy emanating from the same oral cavity
That was responsible in binding them
Celebrating them......

Together forever!

(Page left blank for you to write about a favorite food.)

Chapter 6: What Time Leaves

Retirement

To do or not to do?
It's a word -
Sometimes a double edge sword
This word could be an adjective, a verb, or a noun
But never could it be used as a pronoun.

So, what's this word I wonder
That sets one's mind asunder?
Lights the fire of anticipation in some
While ensuing terrifying thoughts in others to come.

Much time do people spend in preparation
Like it's the ultimate intimation
Of life and death or something more
The contemplation for some can be oftentimes sore.

This word is *retirement*
To define it much time I spent
Is it the withdrawal of participation
In one's occupation?

Or is it the cessation of working
In a job of one's liking?
Is it the stoppage of the bind
Of getting back to the daily grind?

I realized I disliked these definitions
That felt like scary ghostly apparitions
They made less sense as I got closer
To the moment I'd anticipated forever!

Is it paying off mortgages, a debt free space
A healthy nest egg to give you grace
A life of financial freedom adoption
Is it working for fun, when money becomes an option?

The ideas for retirement abounded
With idioms I was surrounded
"She's counting down the days until retirement."
"She's ready to hang up her hat and enjoy retirement."

And there were some more -
"After a successful career, she is now enjoying her newfound freedom."
"He spends his time in retirement volunteering at local charities."
"They are planning to ride off into the sunset after retirement."

I tried counting by day
For my time to hit the hay
But thinking of hanging up my hat
Only made me feel like an ancient bat.

Thoughts of newfound freedom
Volunteering at charities and museum
Filled me with joy and dread
Mixed emotions swimming in my poor head.

I want to be retired, but I don't either
Not ready to be at the end of something neither
And yet the day will come upon me
When a blank sheet is all I see.

Is retirement just reinvention?
When the end becomes the beginning of innovation?
Is it saying goodnight to a venture?
And welcoming sunrise, a new adventure!

What's your own definition of retirement?
Something you can abide with empowerment?
For a physician working 80 hours a week endlessly
Getting to 40 hours may feel like retirement already!

The action of leaving one's office at 5 PM sharp and
ceasing to work until 8 AM
That's halfway to retirement already.
And leaving work at work?
Makes one feel less like a clinical clerk.

Intermittent fasting is trending up
Why not give *intermittent retirement* a bump-up?
Work to rest in an 8:16 ratio
Take a day off midweek to
"Re-wire" on your patio.

Owning your tomorrow
More joy, less sorrow

Someone said-Retirement is when you stop living at work
and start working at living

Now that's a luxurious perk!

A Wrinkly Race

I woke up in a pool of cold sweat,
Ran to the mirror where I was met
By a fifty plus year old face
On which I had dreamed there was a race.

On the blank track and field of the forehead
Parallel lines, from side-to-side spread
The eyelids, like tired runners, a bit droopy.
What's making the smooth cheeks turn so bumpy?

Frown lines leaving vertical furrows
Collagen loss makes little burrows.
Alas!
I have a severe BOTOX deficiency,
Need a doctor ASAP with dermatologic proficiency.

Crow's feet don't cause me shame
"Laugh lines" suit them better by name.
I've carefully collected these wrinkles year by year,
The rat race will guarantee many more lines, not to fear!

A Spade and Wrinkle

It takes guts to call a spade a spade,
It takes courage to call a wrinkle a wrinkle!
Isn't a wrinkle just an entry into the skin's hall of fame?
"Wisdom in motion" on the skin is to blame :-)
A blink of an eyelid and there's one more trophy to spin
Wish I could toss them all at once into a trash-bin
Those pesky wrinkles said it's "No win!"

A Wrinkle, A Pimple, and A Dimple

The anatomy of a wrinkle

Is more complex than a pimple.

Each has its place

At the spectral ends of age.

Why can't Botox turn a wrinkle into a dimple!?

(Page left blank for you to write a short poem showcasing your sense of humor.)

34. 54. or 104.

I am only 54
Sometimes I ask, am I 84?
I’m actually ready to be 94 or even 104!
With friends I feel 24
At work I feel permanently 44
When exercising, I feel 34
So, what am I?
My biological age
Or my chronological age?
Or the age I feel in my mind?

Haiku-Like Lines

God of death
You are the thief of all times
……In plain sight.

(Page left blank for you to write a Haiku on any topic of your choice.)

Dying Well

Dying a slow death
Over my dead body
I'm dying to see you
I'm dying to eat it
It's a dying art
Dying breed
Looking like death warmed over
Death is better than this hell
Death is not the worst thing that can happen to us
Death and taxes
Defying death
Loud enough to wake up the dead
Dia del Muertos
Is dying well an art?

WHY?

I killed that pesky mosquito
But will I get my blood back?
That blood sucking pest
That almost ruined my day
Slaying dragons in dreams
Can be a favorite pastime
Like Harry Potter
I'd like a broom that flies
The mind is so weird
A woman labors for 48 hours
Screaming at the top of her lungs
The outcome is a baby
Pain forgotten, she's ready for the torture again
And sometimes over and over again
How?
Why?

The Unfinished ME

A poem about ME!

I like her a little
I like her not
Sometimes her curly hair drives me crazy
I like her better when she admits her flaws!

She can be funny
But so morose at times
Do not talk to her
On her dysmenorrheal days!

She lives with optimistic passion
Protective about those she loves.
She's minimizing her dislikes
A long journey to learn forgiveness yet to go……

She is not an outward ritualist
But she loves singing Bhajans.
She tries to look inward
With spiritual instincts moving forward.

You can't keep her from dance
Or musical notes for sure
She loves to write daily in i-notes
Be it poetry or prose.

She loves the game of economics
Keenly observing fascinating behavior.
Of humans, animals and birds
Only insecure humans try to hoard money forever……

She loves being a geriatrician
And palliative medicine doc.
Sweet Geri patients tell her cute wise stories
That she loves to write about!
She's awful at Facebooking

She's tweeted once in her life!
She loves old fashioned calls
She's a regular contributor to WhatsApp university :-)

She cares deeply about her family
And friends who've become family
For when the time comes to say goodbye
Her legacy will be
"She wasted no brain cells and lived life to the fullest in rain or shine."

(Left blank for you to write about yourself.)

Idioms of Age

Every poet worth her salt
Must at least once find fault
With the trials and tribulations of growing old
Or be questioned of their creative mold.

Wrinkles and thinning grey hair
Prime targets for poking fun, not fair
Passing wind and slowly transiting bowels
Humor to tackle traitorous organs gives one powers!

Idioms about aging, abound galore
Put on your fun hat, and let's explore
From "coming of age"
To those "senior moments" that pop up on stage.

From "one foot in the grave"
To "old age is not for sissies," be brave
You may be "over the hill"
So, don't forget to make your last will
Who says you cannot teach old dogs' new tricks?????

Old folks can learn to surf Hulu and Net-flix
And Facebook and Instagram and TikTok
Just get over that ageist mental block.
"Age is just a number"
It happens even while you slumber
Exercise, eat right, play with a puppy or kitten
That way, you'll surely stay
"a spring chicken."

Watch out for scammers tracking you all day
After all, "you were not born yesterday."
There is "no fool like an old fool"
Hmmm…... to disprove that idiom, go back to school.
How old would you be if you didn't know
How old you actually are?

Could you pick your own age, how bizarre?!
What do people mean when they say "Act your age?"
Assuming "you're past your prime" is not a good gauge.

Middle age is when the broad mind
And narrow waist change places- someone opined
Old age is when you are finally ready with all the answers
But your kids ask Dr. Google all the questions.

We don't stop playing because we grow old
We grow old because we stop playing, I'm told
Or so said the great George Bernard Shaw
His words put me in a state of awe.

So, play merrily into your "ripe old age"

Feel the joy as you live every page

Aging with grace is an art

Do your part to stay "young at heart!"

(The END)

- or rather the beginning of many more publications from this forever "student" poetess ......goodbye for now!

A Note of Gratitude

Thank you for reading this collection of poetry. Every copy contributes to charitable work, and I hope that impact only exists because YOU chose to open this collection.

In a small but genuine way, these poems belong to something bigger than themselves.

All author profits are donated to organizations fighting hunger, including the ***Feeding America*** *network in the United States and global hunger relief efforts such as the* ***World Food Programme.***

Thank you for YOUR role in being part of that kindness. If this collection meant something to you, please leave a short review on Amazon. Reviews help poetry reach more readers and increase the impact of the charity donation.

- *Neeta*

About the Author

Neeta Nayak grew up in Mysore, India. She was a severely asthmatic child and couldn't run and play like most children. From there to becoming a physician triple boarded in geriatrics, hospice and palliative medicine, she has come a long way.

She's a multiple time recipient of the D magazine's Best Geriatrician award. She is a dedicated geriatrician who finds fulfillment in making home visits to patients with dementia, life-limiting illnesses, and those receiving hospice care.

As a middle schooler, she used to conjure up images of words in her mind but started writing seriously over COVID to cope with the isolation from masking and social distancing.

She is an active member of the Poetry Society of Texas and recently won third prize in a statewide poetry contest and second prize at the Rusk county poetry society contest. She has been published in PULSE- a narrative medicine magazine over a dozen times and written a movie review for the Journal of palliative medicine. Three of her poems have been selected for publication in the Baylor University quarterly journal in 2026.

Neeta was delighted to share the "People's choice award" at the prestigious 2025 and 2026 *Art Meets Poetry* exhibition in McKinney Texas. She is excited about publishing her first collection of poetry and is working on her second – a collection of tales from her geriatric chronicles. She's living her best dream of being a physician with a poetic soul and it is reflected in her Instagram handle "White Coat Poetess."

Authors Statement

I am a physician and “student-poet” with writing in my soul. I love to write and can lose myself in writing for hours at a time. I write about the human faces I see, the joys and sorrows of existence, my relationship with children and cats, the cosmic spirit, the tragedy of death when it occurs in an untimely manner, hospice and its meaning, and multitudes of topics. The sky is not the limit.

Being a physician gives me an intimate glimpse into the lives of many. I learn so very much from my wise elderly patients. It adds fuel and spirit to my creativity. I hope to treasure their knowledge, wisdom and experiences and carry these messages through poetry and essays to my community and empower readers through their highs and lows.

Success may mean different things to different people. For me it is being able to exist in alignment with my goals, wishes and values while making progress in profession and personhood - to stay grounded in purpose even as imagination takes flight.

And the earnest hope to always stay curious about this universe we call home!

Reviewer's Comments

In *Celebration of the Ordinary (and the extraordinary!)*, Neeta Nayak's voice is clear and wondrous. Her precise and distinctive voice is at work on every page. Her poems combine medicine and poetic insight.

Nayak makes observations of her patients braided with humanity.

The poems arrive in different colors like luggage in a carousel in one of her pieces about travel, "The Tumble that Makes Your Heart Rumble!"

There is an immediacy and expectation in Nayak's work.

There are silver linings as well as serious encounters with even more serious matters.

The collection is designed as a workbook as well, with pages for the reader to write their own words. (*This section is left blank for you, the reader, to write a tribute to a person who inspired and empowered you*!) and *(Page left blank intentionally for you to write a few words on living life brightly!)* are two examples.

The titles are delightful. "Mermaid in Cancun." "The Kit-Kat Santa." "The White Coat Fashionista." "Buffalo Hump and Moon Face." Even a made-up word, "Porange," is a surprise.

Celebration of the Ordinary (and the extraordinary!) is an excellent read. The way it should be.

-- Diane Glancy
Piece and *The Cubist and the Lost Notebooks of the Painter's Wife*

www.ingramcontent.com/pod-product-compliance
Lightning Source LLC
LaVergne TN
LVHW010938110826
845149LV00013B/2649

* 9 7 9 8 9 9 4 3 3 7 1 0 3 *